The Whisper Within

Irene Martinez

Presentation by *BookLeaf Publishing*

Web: www.bookleafpub.com

E-mail: info@bookleafpub.com

ISBN: 9789357440943

First edition 2023

DEDICATION

This book I dedicate to God, Christ, my daughter, Aleyna, my husband Eddy Cruz and to my Tino Viera. RIP.

My Mind on E

I stare down at my donut, raspberry filling.

"What's this empty feeling"?

Can pastry ever be enough or even fulfilling?

Emotions, I will forever hold inside.

Madness and sadness are what I hide.

Love that I found and I would die,
contemplating many times of suicide.

I had lost love that meant to me the most.

He left without leaving a note.

He lost it and loose self-control.

He left me and this ugly cruel world.

I will never see him grow old.

A low life, living on the fast high life.

 A deep affliction.

My downfall leading me to prescription and addiction.

A living lie that made me want to die.

It Isolated and solitude myself.

I know deep I did not want to kill myself

Hoping to discover the self.

It reveals an ideal to heal.

To change the thought of mind and to stop being logic and be real.

To kill ego and be born again.

He in the spiritual

 I, in the physical.

My life being a painting and I am curious of the mystical.

The mystical involved with the metaphysical.

I know I will soon find peace.

I will complete it and it will be my masterpiece.

My Karmic Debt

Up from a nightmare.

I was scared cause you were there.

My memories my heart cannot forget.

My karmic debt.

We, both wanting to find the love and attention.

Us, both not knowing how to express the affection.

At times, I still believed, you would come back to
me.

Why did you abandoned me?

Did you even love me?

Why did you hurt me?

Did I ever come up in your dreams?

Did I once ever come up in your thoughts?

Wondering if once ever missed me?

Why did you hurt me?

I was tricked and put in such conflict.

Feelings I could not adjust with, and I lost my mind.

I went mental.

It covered my eyes and I stayed blind.

I did not know how to be soft or gentle.

"How could you be so selfish and die?"

"Why did you give up and not give it enough time?"

To see if I could of fixed you.

I will never love again!

Instead, it wounded and ruin me!

My heart alive, and it still bleeds.

Used and abused, and it still beats.

How much more can I take?

Everything being a mistake.

I am done!

I'm done looking for a soulmate.

Till Next Lifetime

I can't sleep, wishing you were beside me.

All I do is weep.

The pain that had me weak.

Your company is what I seek.

He was the one.

The man of my dreams.

How I hate mental disease!

I will always remember you.

Do not worry for me?

Lay and rest in peace.

Yet, I hear in my head, that your not dead.

You alive and flesh is what had died.

Letting go of discourage.

Becoming a fighter, will build my courage.

I will overcome my fears.

The ones I've had within for many years.

Until the next life time.

Keeping seeking the light.

Together in Heaven forever.

Sleep well and good night.

I love you, always and forever.

His Dream

You were a beautiful dream.

Everyone's cup of tea.

Captured by her eyes and beauty.

She was art to me.

What a delicacy!

The greatest piece to me.

I gave her a kiss.

One last kiss, I know I would miss.

Awaken by God, and she is in my thoughts.

I know she misses me.

She wouldn't know where I will be.

Forgive me.

I need to reach the end of the tunnel.

I am on the path of the dark night.

I wanted to end my suffering.

Each day, I am recovering.

She was painting at the same time foretelling.

For I knew, somehow the story she was telling.

The gallery of our memories.

Her soul making melodies.

A remembrance that brought my presence.

She painted when she wept.

Old brushes that she kept.

Her colors' aspect bring up beautiful effects.

I also painted one for you.

Hoping you got the one I sent.

Vital Forces

Why do we think like we do?
Holding on to what feels true.
Beliefs and thoughts that comes from the
subconscious mind.
What will you find?

Theories of the planets and galaxies.
Dreams and fantasies.
Ideas and illusions.

The sense of self.
The devil being the air that wanders out there.
What he wants is your despair.
He wants you to unaware.
He doesn't care.
He will not be fair.
God, only one that can spare.

Spiritual vital forces that come from different
sources.
What could this be?
I tend to listen to words that come from a distant.
What is God, telling me?
I have not heard his voice in a long time.
The way it sounds, it sounds like mine.

It tells me to become pure.
To fight temptation and stay persistent.
Be grateful of life.
Be like Christ.
To open my heart and my eyes.
He will be removing one of the veils.
I would then understand self.

Oh, how the dark forces were deceiving me.
It got the best of me.
Losing the one I love was a defeat.
I do not feel weak.
Regaining my power for Jesus Christ is in me.

Divine Feminine

Since the beginning of time love existed.

The two thinking of flesh.

How can they get this twisted?

The woman wanting to caress.

The man wants to get her undressed.

To reproduce his seed in the flower.

He wanted to empower.

What happen to the love of the mother?

She seeking a man that has honor and is proper.

When did the children become a bother?

Having many babies and leaving their scholar.

How can we show love to one another?

When it wasn't teached to the father or mother.

These times have changed.

The divine feminine estranged.

It was there evasion.

Women wanting to obtain independence and
liberation.

The people have evolved.

Woman afraid to open to love.

It was the world that made me.

What has become of us?

All is lust and there is no trust.

Love is not what is on the skin.

It is what is inside.

We need to treat our mothers like queens.

Women encourage your men like kings.

Love is not what it seems.

It's beyond everything.

Even the angels sing.

Flying up to heaven with their wings.

For they know love.

The unconditional love of God.

What is Purgatory?

As I walk the shadows, I hear the cries of the dead.

I hear children, men and women.

Crying, begging and praying to be heard.

The Divine Comedy story.

The three-mirror experiment.

My heart hurts for their torment.

Spiritual realm on the ethereal plane.

The saints were also there.

Souls who stayed wicked and others sickened.

Souls that live in the trees, plants and in the dirt.

Observing and analyzing everything I could see.

Why is this happening to me?

The walls transcending becoming pitch black.

I kept walking a notice something coming from the back.

A dim amber light.

The closer the light came to me, it became white.

I paid close attention, a fairy.

She was dancing in delight.

I started to follow this mystic fly.

Aware of everything I was walking by.

Remember what you see.

It is not a dream.

I heard sounds and I saw a mouse come from the ground.

The mouse becoming a hound.

Then all the animals started shape-shifting all around.

I saw lizards, lions, bears and horses to seeing dogs, cats and birds.

What is the meaning of all this?

Following her light keeping her close to my sight.

She suddenly went into the window.

How?

I decided to peek inside.

I saw the saints falling from Heaven.

I saw the Jacob's ladder.

Where the angels where ascending and descending.

Titans and Nephilims roaming Earth.

Time going back.

History replaying itself.

Bringing the gods from the mythology stories.

The Aquarian Age leading us back to the barbaric times.

Over The Rainbow

"Follow the yellow brick road",
Taking us to "there is no place like home".
Words that show up in my head,
Playing like a song on rewind.
I take a deep breath.
Closed my eyes and cleared my mind.
Meditating and connecting to my higher self.
When I felt this warm sensation.
Light codes that brought information.

"Your body is your temple, always come here to connect.
You need to use your body, mind, and spirit to reflect.
Have courage, an open heart and use your brain to discern
what is correct.
The Golden Path, that leads to God and the Holy Spirit.
You need to grow spiritually like a flower.
Be grounded like a rock for mental power.
Somewhere over the rainbow.
The bridge to Heaven on Earth".

Father, please forgive us.
Forgive me! for I separated myself from you.
You were always with me.
The voice inside my head.
I am so pleased.

You put me on ease.
I will follow you.
I will tell people about you.

"Heal yourself.
Physical, emotional and mental.
Use your magic ruby red slippers, the root that that helps
you find yourself.
Connecting the thousand petals.
The purple flower called Soma.
The elixir, the healing with a beautiful aroma.
A secret you need to acknowledge, for it carries
knowledge.
Where you can find Emerald City.
The sacred and pure heart.
What is it telling you?
Where is it guiding and you?
Somewhere over the rainbow.
Heaven on Earth.
I am the truth and the way.
You will see".

Lord, I will do as you command.
I will serve others, if that is what you demand.
Thank you, my God, for I needed this for my salvation.
If others could see what you did for me?
I will help them to also believe.
Thank you, for confining in me.

Words of Wisdom

"Wake up! Wake up!"

The angels awaken me.

Would you look at the time?

You are blind for you cannot see.

The time is coming up.

Do you see the times we are in now?

"Wake up!"

"Foolish and selfish people!

All you have done is sin.

What have you done during this lifetime?

My people, all of you gave in.

They do not talk to me or repent for their sins.

Surrender before Judgement.

No one knowing the day it will come.

The day the thief enters your home.

God, only knows the outcome.

You will not have any more time.

Save humanity.

Save yourselves, so your not the one panicking.

Keep faith strong and change mentality.

Change your perception on vitality.

God is coming.

Alive or dead.

It has been said".

God is Love

It's is God and me only.
I wake up and I do not feel lonely.
I am putting my trust in God.
He is the only one I got.

Remind me, Father.
You in control and it is at your pace.
Provide me your light and shine it on my face.

Forgive me, for I still have pain from my heart.

Loosing someone was hard and I fell apart.

But now I am found.

I am ready to start.

I am leaving the past.

Yet, I already said my goodbyes.

Lost time to feel like I came back just in time.

Right back on time to the finish line.

Lord, I can not do this without you.

I will be lost in my mind and thought.

For this is the love I seeked.

The love that I fought.

You never forgotten of me.

Your love, I now see!

A strong desire to go toward this direction.

Leading me to you and your perfection.

Life being a moment.

Life being a memory.

God, I know with you I belong.

I will wait for you.

I do not care for how long.

In the meantime, I will write you another poem

I will write you a song.

The Greatest Commandment

The greatest love that our God has for us.

Bless, Jesus Christ for he died for us.

Love that conquers all.

Removing the bandages of sin that is in all.

Merciful, kind and pure.

A deep affection that can cure.

Do not be confused, for God's love is not to be feared.

So, why do we fear then?

God is everywhere and He is with us.

He is real and he is not dead.

Fear the Lord of not knowing him.

Fear of not loving him.

Why don't you just stop and listen?

He will sometimes take his time to answer back.

Believe me, it take time and patience.

Ask him a question, without hesitation.

It takes a lot of dedication.

He wants your friendship.

Build the relationship

FOLLOW YOU

God, I want to obey you in everything I do.

I want to follow every commandment you have.

I want to be strong from temptation and evil too.

I want to be righteous and give it all I have.

You are so good, my father.

Your kind and merciful, my Lord.

Lead me closer to you and push Satan farther.

Your word is what it is, a double edged sword.

My king, teach me to be a servant of love.

Fill me heart with your words, enlighten it.

My Savior

God, you are my bright star that lights up when it gets dark
God, you are like the sea, bringing tranquility to my ark
You are the refreshing winds that bring me back home
God, for you, I long.

You are truly divine
Sweet like wine, coming from grape vines
A beautiful rose and I want to make you mine
Your love is patient, gentle, faithful and kind
I will always be seeking, your always on my mind

I will go find you in the trees
I will find you with the birds
I know I can find you in the breeze
I know I can find you in all the wonders of the world

Lord, I seek your peace
I seek your protection.

Cosmic Lovers

I want to talk about my best friend.
We has a soul recognition moment.
We were pulled together without appointment.
My friend who came to save me from my own
mind's torment.

He felt like Heaven sent.
I still remember the day we met.
It was God's intention.
Unaware of all the signs, I should of paid more
attention.

He was like me.
He was spiritual like me.
It captivated and intrigued me.
Feeling like this is too good to be true.
Who would of knew?

Can this really last forever?
A fear of rejection.
When I told myself I would never.
A fear of deception.

When I fell.
He went down that rabbit hill as well.

God in him found him and he saved me.
The look in his face, like please trust me?

Blood contaminated with love potion.
A strong emotional connection.
To shine together, to be faithful and honest.
The commitment and devotion.
Can I really pour my light to this human soul?
To be united with God in one soul.
Can I trust again?
Can I really, ever love again?

Intervene

A female warrior to the Lord.

He was a King that serve God.

You are my Adam, I am your Eve.

Divine love.

Intervene from the one from above.

A man who loved God!

Reminding me of the one time.

In the Garden of Eden.

The man I one prayed for at night.

I was scared and hid from him.

I can't love again.

My best friend, how would this end?

I don't want to loose this friendship.

How our souls connected together in this
dimension.

It became strong and with tension.

What was seeking you, had already seeked you.

My twin, my yang, my soulmate.

Who fell in love with me!

Who accepted me and my mini me?

Who never gave up and never lost faith in me!

Now, everyone will know our names.

But loving God more that money or fame.

I will die with you.

Lay next to you.

And in Heaven, I pray to be with you.

Children of God

Teach the kids about ME.
Let them know my son's name.
Tell them of He.
Jesus Christ, is the name.

I will listen to you, my children.
Talk to Me, every day and all day.
Pray to Me, my children.
Believe in Me, I am the way

Tell me your worries.
Tell me your sins.
I already took care them,
but continue to repent of them.
I want the sincere you.
I know when you are being true.

Our kids are our future.
Let them have something they can lean on.
Let them know I am real.
They will know for sure.
When they notice my signs.

Have faith in me.
Even if you do not see me.

Pray for the children.
Do not let them separate them from me.
It's your legacy and it starts with the father.
So, I tell God is father.
He encourages you to go farther.
Do not be afraid.
I'm from beyond, and further.

The Power of Jesus, name!

Jesus!!

Commander in Chief, hoo rah!
He is our Salvation.
Accept him in your life.
" I accept Jesus Christ, today."
I believe he is the water to my life.

"Ask and you will receive"
The power of the words.
They send energy and vibrations.
Words with light and frequency.

Imagine then, Jesus, name.
What you can do with his name?!

We need to show the love
Show it with kind words.
Love from above.
Destroy the chaos of the worlds.

We create and send energy.
Let us send enlightenment.
We can save the world.
Be the empowerment.
Let you light be bright!!

Be giving and be open to receive.

Marry Me!

Our soul is always on a quest.
It voyages to the East.
It has traveled to the West.
A challenge to bring out the best.

My soul on a journey.
Seeking someone to understand me.
Looking for one man, from so many.
A partner I can share my company.

The friend that I need.
A man that to him family was important then money.
A brother that I confined in and be play like we were kids.
Childlike, laughing because we were so funny.

God being our teacher.
All day and night listening to each other.
My protector like a father and healed me like a doctor.

I also know God is all we need.
His company we also seek.
The companion with us all week.
Should I say more or less?
Let the people assume and guess.

Eddy, will you marry me?
To become my husband.
Will you take my hand?
And come with me?